Schools Library and Information Services

S00000640246

Materials

Metal

Chris Oxlade

www.heinemann.co.uk/library
Visit our website to find out more information about Heinemann Library books.

To Order:
 Phone 44 (0) 1865 888066
 Send a fax to 44 (0) 1865 314091
Visit the Heinemann Library Bookshop at www.heinemann.co.uk/library to browse our catalogue and order online.

First published in Great Britain by Heinemann Library, Halley Court, Jordan Hill, Oxford OX2 8EJ,
a division of Reed Educational and Professional Publishing Ltd.
Heinemann is a registered trademark of Reed Educational and Professional Publishing Ltd.

OXFORD MELBOURNE AUCKLAND JOHANNESBURG BLANTYRE
GABORONE IBADAN PORTSMOUTH (NH) USA CHICAGO

© Reed Educational and Professional Publishing Ltd 2002
The moral right of the proprietor has been asserted.

All rights reserved. No part of this publication may be reproduced, stored in a retrieval system, or transmitted in any form or by any means, electronic, mechanical, photocopying, recording or otherwise, without either the prior written permission of the publishers or a licence permitting restricted copying in the United Kingdom issued by the Copyright Licensing Agency Ltd, 90 Tottenham Court Road, London W1P 0LP.

Designed by Storeybooks
Originated by Dot Gradations Ltd
Printed by South China Printing in Hong Kong/China

ISBN 0 431 03742 6 (hardback)　　　　ISBN 0 431 03747 7 (paperback)
06 05 04 03 02　　　　　　　　　　　　06 05 04 03 02
10 9 8 7 6 5 4 3 2 1　　　　　　　　　　10 9 8 7 6 5 4 3 2 1

British Library Cataloguing in Publication Data
　　　Oxlade, Chris
　　　Metal. – (Materials)
　　　1. Metal
　　　I. Title
　　　620.1'6

...LEY PUBLIC LIBRARIES
L　46200
640246　　SCH
J669

Acknowledgements
Corbis /Peter Johnson p.16, /Paul A.Souders p.14, /Yogi Inc. p.15; D.I.Y. Photo Library p.23, /Photodisc p.24; Edifice p.7; Photodisc pp.6, 17, 19; PPL Library p.11; Rolls Royce PLC p.25; Still Pictures /David Drain p.27, /Mark Edwards pp 12, 13, 26, /Thomas Raupach pp.4, 29; Stone p.18; Tudor Photography pp.5, 22; Zul Mukhida p.8.

Cover photograph reproduced with permission of Tudor Photography.

Every effort has been made to contact copyright holders of any material reproduced in this book. Any omissions will be rectified in subsequent printings if notice is given to the publishers.

Contents

You can find words shown in bold, **like this**, in the glossary.

What is metal?

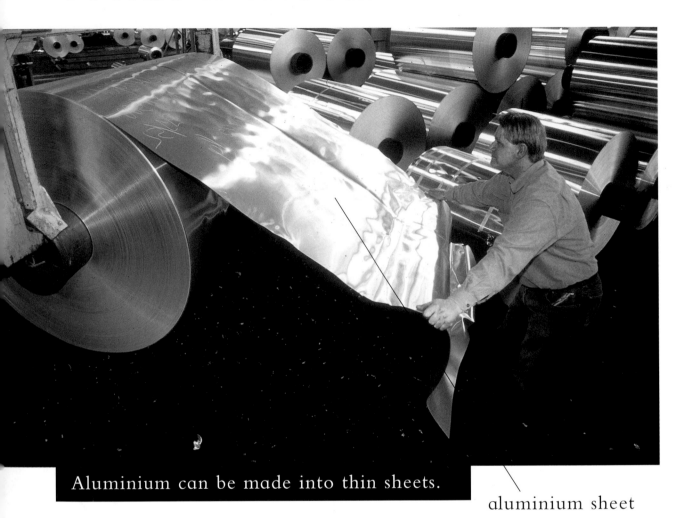

Aluminium can be made into thin sheets.

aluminium sheet

There are dozens of different metals. Metals are found in rocks in the ground. The metal in the photo is aluminium. It has just been made into thin sheets.

There is more aluminium in the Earth's crust than any other metal.

People make many useful things from metals. They are called metal objects.

All these things are made from metal.

grater

tankard

bowl

saucepan

cutlery

toast rack

pastry cutters

screws

chain

Hard and soft

About 766 million tonnes of raw steel are made around the world every year.

steel blade

This saw has a steel blade.

Some metals are very hard and very strong.
It is difficult to cut and bend them. The cutting
edge, or blade, of this **saw** is made of a very hard
metal called **steel**.

Some metals, such as lead, are softer and quite weak. It is easy to cut or bend them. In some countries, builders use strips of lead on roofs.

Lead is the softest of the commonly used metals.

roof

lead strip

The lead strips on this roof keep water out.

Electricity and heat

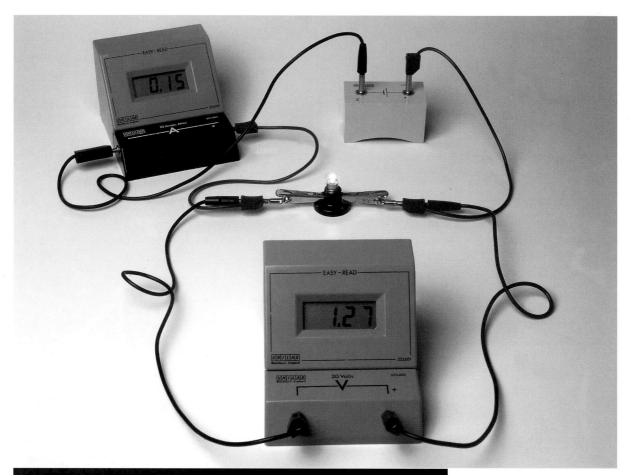

Electricity flows through the wires in this **circuit**.

Most metals let **electricity** flow through them easily. They are good **conductors** of electricity. The **lightbulb** glows when electricity flows through the metal in the wires.

Metals are also good at letting heat flow through them. They are called good conductors of heat.

Metal pans let heat flow from the cooking ring to the food inside.

food

metal pan

cooking ring

Metals and magnets

magnet

This magnet is so large it needs a machine to lift it.

Some metal things stick to **magnets**. At this rubbish dump, a massive magnet is being used to pick the metal objects out of the pile of other rubbish.

magnet

steel cans

One end of a magnet is called its north pole and the other end is its south pole.

These steel cans stick to the magnet.

The only everyday metals that stick to magnets are **iron** and **steel**. Paper clips are made of steel. So are many cans. Most metals do not stick to magnets.

Where metals come from

rock

digger

Huge diggers load the broken rocks on to trucks.

Metals are found in some rocks in the ground. The rocks are called **ores**. Miners break up the rocks with tools and **explosives**.

Look at the picture again. Iron ore gives this land a rust-red colour.

The rock is worked on to get the metal out.
This is called processing. To get **iron** from iron
ore, the ore is **melted** in a hot **furnace**.

furnace   molten iron

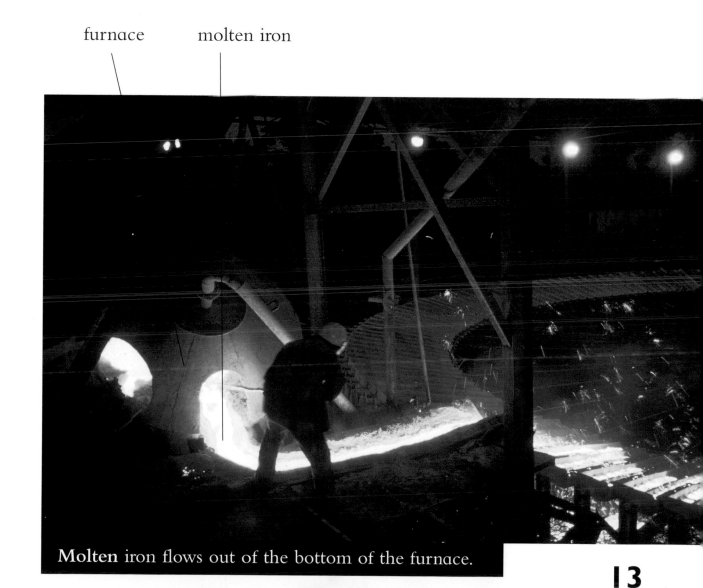

Molten iron flows out of the bottom of the furnace.

Shaping metals

Metals can be bent and hammered to make different shapes. This blacksmith heats **iron** until it glows red to make it soft. Then he shapes it by hitting it with a hammer.

Red-hot iron can be hammered into different shapes.

blacksmith

furnace

hammer

iron

anvil

The blacksmith hammers the iron on a block called an anvil.

14

Metals can also be cut into shapes with tools such as **drills** and **saws**. The parts of the tools that do the cutting are made from very hard metals.

drill bit

Sometimes special drills are used to cut holes in metal.

drill

Rusting

car body

rust

Rust is destroying this car's bodywork.

If **iron** or **steel** things are left out in the wet, they go brown and flaky. The iron slowly turns into a new material called **rust**. Metals such as gold and silver stay shiny because they do not rust.

Rust damages iron and steel things. It makes them crumble. You can stop things going rusty by painting them, or by coating them with another metal called zinc. This stops water getting through.

This watering can has been coated with zinc to stop it from rusting.

Metals for electricity

copper wires

Cables like these, which carry **electricity** around a house, have wires in them. The wires are made of copper. The cables are covered in plastic to stop the electricity getting from one wire to another.

plastic casings

electricity cable

Did you know that copper was the first metal to be used regularly by humans to make tools?

Copper is mainly used to make electrical wire.

Inside machines such as computers, electricity travels along thin copper tracks on a plastic board. A metal called **solder** can be used to fix the parts, or components, to the board.

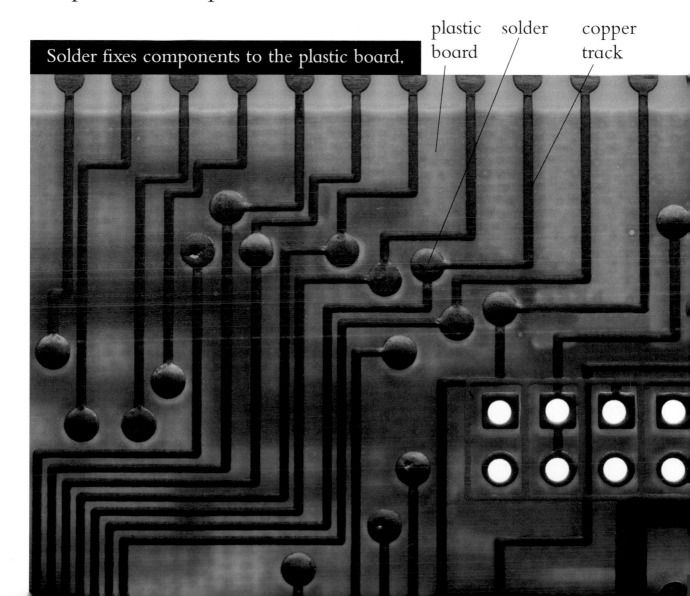

Solder fixes components to the plastic board.

plastic board

solder

copper track

Iron and steel

This drain cover is made of cast iron.

drain cover   road

Iron is the most common metal we use. It is shaped by **melting** it and pouring it into moulds. This is called casting, and the iron is called cast iron.

steel frame

builder

steel spirit level

The first steel-framed building was built in 1885!

This building has a steel frame.

Steel is made from iron mixed with tiny amounts of other materials. It is much stronger than iron. Many things, such as tools, cars and the frames that hold some buildings up, are made from steel.

Aluminium and copper

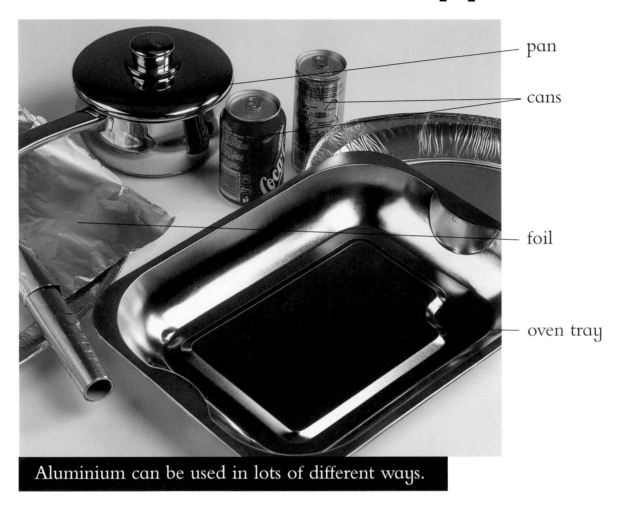

pan

cans

foil

oven tray

Aluminium can be used in lots of different ways.

The thin foil used to wrap food in the kitchen is made of a metal called aluminium. Aluminium is lighter than **iron** or **steel**. It is also used to make cooking pans and some cans.

22

Copper is a reddish-brown metal used to make the wire in **electricity** cables. Water pipes are made from copper, too, because it does not go rusty like iron or steel.

These pipes are made of copper.

Look around your house and see if there are water pipes made of copper.

copper pipes

Alloys

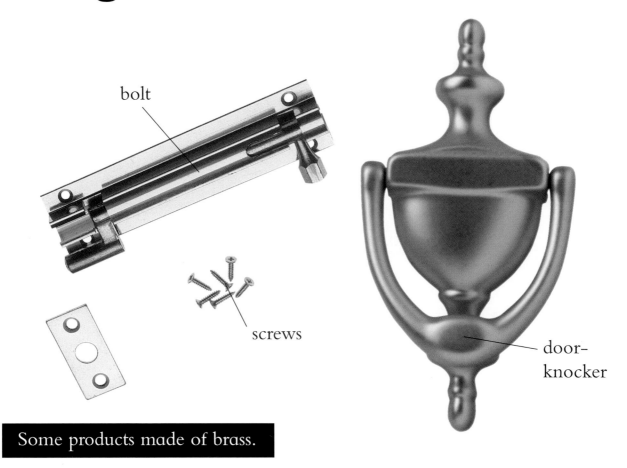

bolt

screws

door-knocker

Some products made of brass.

An **alloy** is a metal made by mixing two or more metals together. Alloys are harder and stronger than the metals they are made from. Brass is an alloy of copper and zinc.

Aeroplane builders use alloys that are very strong but very light in weight. Aeroplane bodies and engines are made from alloys that contain metals called aluminium, nickel and titanium.

jet engine fan

Jet engines are made using strong, light metals.

Recycling metals

car   truck

Old vehicles are often sent to scrap yards for crushing.

A lot of the rubbish we throw away is made of metal. It takes a lot of **energy** to make metals. This energy is wasted if the metals are thrown away.

Most metals can be used again, or recycled, instead of being thrown away. If people throw old metal things into special bins, the metal can be collected. Then it is **melted** down and made into new things.

Used drinks cans are collected, crushed and recycled.

crushed cans

Fact file

Most metals are hard, shiny materials.

Metals feel smooth and cold.

Some metals are very hard and very strong. Some metals are softer and weaker.

All metals allow **electricity** to flow through them.

Alloys, such as solder, bronze and brass, are made from other metals.

All metals allow heat to flow through them.

Iron and **steel** are metals that stick to **magnets**. Most metals do not stick to magnets.

Most metals do not float.

Would you believe it?

These lumps of gold are called nuggets. The largest gold nugget ever found weighed an amazing 70 kilograms. That's as heavy as a full-grown person!

Gold nuggets are sometimes found in rock.

gold nuggets

Glossary

a b c d e f g h i j k l m n o p q r s t u v w x y z

alloy   metal made by mixing two metals

circuit   set of wires joined together for electricity to flow through

conductor   material that lets electricity or heat flow through it

drill   tool for making holes in pieces of material

electricity   form of energy. We use electricity to make electric machines work.

energy   energy is needed to make things happen. For example, you need energy to move about.

explosive   something that explodes, or blows up, when it is heated

factory   place where things are made using machines

furnace   container, like a huge oven, inside which materials are melted

iron   shiny, grey metal used to make millions of different objects

melt   turn from solid to liquid

magnet   object that attracts iron or steel

molten   solid material that is heated until it melts

ore   rock that metals are found in. It is dug from the ground.

rust   brown, flaky material that appears on iron or steel when it is left in the wet. We then say that the iron or steel is rusty.

solder   alloy, often made of copper and zinc. It is used to join electrical parts.

steel   metal made mostly from iron. Steel is stronger than iron.

More books to read

Science All Around Me: Materials by Karen Bryant-Mole Heinemann Library, 1996

Science Explorers: Metal, A & C Black, 2000

Science Files: Metal by Steve Parker, Heinemann Library 2001

Shooting Stars: Material Matter by Robert Roland, Belitha Press, 2002

Index